Finding Out About
WOMEN IN
NINETEENTH-CENTURY
BRITAIN

Madeline Jones

B.T. Batsford Limited, *London*

Contents

Typeset by Tek-Art Ltd, Kent
and printed in Great Britain by
R J Acford
Chichester, Sussex
for the publishers
B.T. Batsford Limited,
4 Fitzhardinge Street
London W1H 0AH

ISBN 0 7134 5049 5

Cover illustrations

The colour photograph is from the painting "Too Early" by James Tissot (*Guildhall Library/Bridgeman Art Library*); the advertisement comes from *Black's Guide to South Wales*; the right-hand engraving shows women factory workers in the pen-grinding room (*Mansell Collection*).

Frontispiece

"Ladies Outside the Church". This picture illustrated a story in a religious magazine of the 1870s.

ACKNOWLEDGMENTS

The Author and Publishers would like to thank the following for permission to reproduce illustrations: BBC Hulton Picture Library for pages 20 and 24; Mansell Collection for page 40 (right); Oxfordshire Central Library for page 33; The Science Museum for page 37 (bottom); Wolverhampton Central Library for page 16; York Castle Museum for page 36. Thanks also go to the Girls' Public Day School Trust for permission to reproduce the extract from the memories of Mrs Ethel Palmer quoted in *G.P.D.S.T. 1872-1972: A Centenary Review* on page 32.

Introduction

A modern girl would notice many differences in her way of life if she suddenly found herself back in the nineteenth century. Her clothes, if she were rich enough, might be pretty, but she would find them very uncomfortable. She would be less well educated than her brothers and her life when she grew up would be much more limited than theirs. Two things might particularly surprise her: women did not have political rights (no women could vote in elections for M.P.s) and they were looked on by most people as being quite incapable of thinking or talking about serious matters. Even when, in the last part of the century, there was more support for the view that women should be better educated and encouraged to share men's interests, a progressive magazine, *The Young Englishwoman*, could still suggest:

> **Mental culture should not, and does not as a rule, rob woman of her womanliness, nor render her less lovable. A husband might encourage his wife in a suitable choice of reading matter. He could read the paper aloud to her while she darns his socks.**

Boys were looked on as more important than girls. Here an only son has just come home from boarding school in 1872. How many sisters has he, and how are they treating him? Who are the two women on the right?

Some women, all through the century, did great things in spite of all these limitations. Florence Nightingale broke away from a boring family life in a rich home to nurse the sick and to become a national heroine in the Crimean War (1854-6). Women like Jane Austen, Charlotte, Emily and Anne Brontë and George Eliot wrote novels which are still read and enjoyed today. (Notice though that "George" Eliot took a man's name. She was really Marian Evans. The Brontë sisters also wrote under men's names at first: why, do you think?) In ordinary families, too, the life of the women varied. In mining areas like South Wales the mother of the family had a very strong position and often took charge of the men's wages. However, as you'll see, women generally had to struggle against the idea that they were less clever and less important than men.

Another very big difference between modern and nineteenth-century life, both for men and women, was the gulf between people from different backgrounds and social groups. Women were not equal with men, but they were not equal with each other either. Some were "ladies", usually from families rich enough to keep them, so that they did not have to consider earning a living, and with plenty of servants, so that they never needed to do housework. (Some "ladies" were poor, but they were wives or daughters of men either once rich, or else well-educated.) The rest were just "women". A "lady" stood out by her manners and by her appearance. She often had little idea of how other women lived. The writer Virginia Woolf, born in 1882, summed up the contrasts between the life of ladies like herself and other women when she wrote an introduction to a collection of working women's life stories published in 1931 – *Life As We Have Known It*:

> **One could not be Mrs Giles of Durham because one's body had never stood at the wash-tub; one's hands had never wrung and scrubbed and chopped up**

whatever the meat may be that makes a miner's supper . . . . One sat in an armchair or read a book . . . there were no armchairs . . . or hot water laid on in their [the working women's] lives . . . . Bakers and butchers did not call for orders. They did not sign a cheque to pay the weekly bills . . . . They did not stroll through the house and say, that cover must go to the wash, or those sheets need changing. They plunged their arms in hot water and scrubbed the clothes themselves . . .

Of course there are still differences between the way rich and poor people live today, but you could have an interesting discussion about the ways in which the gap between rich and poor women has narrowed (Virginia Woolf herself was the daughter and wife of professional men – not of noblemen or millionaires).

You will find examples of all kinds of women in this book. Even so, in a short book like this one we can only give you a sample of the huge amount of material which tells us how women lived in nineteenth-century Britain. You will enjoy finding more for yourselves.

◀ A poor village woman meets the lady of the manor – the local landowner's wife – at the church door. Notice the difference in dress and the older woman's respectful curtsey.

Useful Sources

1. PEOPLE TO ASK
a) *The Librarian* of your local public library will be able to suggest books on this topic and can also tell you whether there is any unpublished material, like memoirs or diaries, in the local history section of the library.
b) *Older friends and relatives* may have family stories to tell. Though very few people can now remember the nineteenth century themselves, more can remember being told about the lives of their own parents or grandparents.

2. VISUAL MATERIAL
a) You may be able to find family photographs from the nineteenth century. Your local library may also have collections of old photographs as well as paintings (sometimes *by* women as well as *of* women).
b) In museums you can often find examples of nineteenth-century costume: if you are very lucky you may know someone who has kept some clothes from this period.
c) Some nineteenth-century articles tell us a lot about women's lives. Look for washtubs and scrubbing-boards and mangles in museums: in junk shops you can still sometimes find cheap flat-irons or button-hooks for doing up buttoned gloves and boots. See if you can collect enough things for a classroom museum.
d) Victorian books, often very well illustrated, can be bought cheaply in charity shops or jumble sales if you keep a good look out for them. Their covers, as well as the pictures and stories inside, are interesting.

3. WRITTEN SOURCES
a) *Diaries and letters* Your reference library may have nineteenth-century diaries or letters written by local women. You can also look for these in your County Archives' Catalogue. (Kent County Archives, for example, has a wonderful Victorian diary kept by

a girl called Eva Knatchbull Hugessen.) If you want to visit your County Archives, in the Record Office in your county town, always contact the County Archivist first to make an appointment.

b) *Newspapers and magazines* Ask your reference library if they have nineteenth-century copies of local newspapers: these contain fascinating advertisements as well as stories. Many libraries have old copies of church magazines, and you can sometimes find bound copies of nineteenth-century magazines in charity or second-hand bookshops.

c) *Directories* Local town and county directories give lists of shopkeepers and some list the occupations of people living in the different streets. You can track down the main occupations of women in your area. Directories also often contain advertisements, some with illustrations.

d) *Census material* Your reference library may have copies of the original answers to Victorian census questions – the Census Returns. From 1851 these give occupation and place of birth for everyone in the area: they also show size of families, number of servants in a house and age of each person. At present you can only see the census details up to 1881, because this private information is not made public for 100 years after the census is taken.

e) *School log-books* These records kept by head-teachers give useful details about women teachers and girl pupils. They are often kept in libraries or county Record Offices.

f) *Parliamentary papers* Your nearest large library may have nineteenth-century copies of *Hansard*, containing a record of debates in Parliament, like debates on whether to give women the vote. There are also many collections of extracts from parliamentary committees' reports, etc., with details of women's working conditions. Some of these are listed on p. 47.

g) *Poor Law records* The *Minute Books* and other records of the Boards of Guardians, who were responsible for helping the poor after 1834, have much information about poor women. Your local library may have some of these records. If not, try the County Archives.

See what you can find out about late nineteenth-century ladies' lives from this 1886 advertisement (you'll notice at least one difference in fashion between then and now if you read the small print).

Growing Up

Childhood ended early for poor girls. In rich families, however, girls of 16 or 17 were considered to be still "in the schoolroom".

MISTRESS OF THE HOUSE

J.M. Barrie, who wrote *Peter Pan*, came from a poor Scottish family. His mother, born in the early part of the century, hardly had a childhood at all.

She was eight when her mother's death made her mistress of the house and mother to her little brother, and from that time she scrubbed and mended and baked and sewed . . . and she carried the water from the pump, and had her washing-days and her ironings and a stocking always on the wire for odd moments . . . (J.M. Barrie, *Margaret Ogilvy*, 1896)

Look at the joke under the picture: what are the three sisters talking about? Can you find the youngest – the one who has not yet "come out" of the schoolroom into the grown-up world? (One of the signs of being grown-up was when a girl put up her long hair, instead of wearing it loose on her shoulders.)

BARE NECESSARIES.

No. 1 (having her hair done). "PAPA SAYS HE WON'T HEAR OF MY MARRYING WITHOUT A HOUSE IN TOWN?"

No. 2 (at Tea). "AND MAMMA SAYS I'M NOT TO THINK OF ANYONE WHO HAS NOT A MOOR IN SCOTLAND, AND A HUNTING-BOX AT MELTON."

No. 3 (not yet "come out"). "WELL! *I* SHOULD NOT DREAM OF MARRYING ANYONE WHO CAN'T AFFORD *ALL THREE!*"

CHAPERONS

As you can see, it was not thought proper for young ladies to be alone with men who were not their relations. An older lady, called a chaperon, stayed with the girl if a young man called or went with her to parties or the theatre. *Punch* magazine made fun of girls' feelings about chaperons in 1889, quoting the view of *The Lady* magazine that the custom was dying out.

RULES FOR UNMARRIED DAUGHTERS

Wealthy girls were strictly supervised. They were not supposed to form friendships with men unless their parents knew and approved. They were certainly not supposed to marry without their parents' consent, even if they were over 21. Lady Caroline Capel was very upset when her eldest daughter, Harriet, a young woman of 22, fell in love and kept this a secret. The Capels were living in Brussels at the time, and Lady Caroline wrote to reassure her own mother that she did not allow her daughters too much freedom:

> ... those people who know us all, are always asking, "Why is Lady Caroline so *Very* particular? ...". I early saw the sort of Place this was & that certain restrictions were necessary ... what would you say if you heard of Your Grand-daughters riding out without Father, brother or Chaperon of any kind with five or six young Men? ... Or if you heard of them walking in the Public walks arm in arm with men & without any chaperon with them? ...
> (Lady Caroline Capel to Lady Uxbridge, 19 April, 1815, quoted in Marquess of Anglesey, ed., *The Capel Letters*, 1955)

Harriet's love-letters were discovered, and her father fought a duel with the man concerned. Luckily, no one was hurt, and eventually Harriet married someone else.

My dear Mr Punch, I must shout Hip!
           Hurrah!
You really don't know how delighted
           we are,
To read there's a prospect, at no distant
           day,
Of ending the grim chaperonical sway:
When girls will be able to do as they
           please,
With no one to counsel, or worry, or
           tease!
When I may sit talking with *Someone*
           alone,
Unmindful of frowns from a prim
           Chaperon!

If I'm at the Play, in the smartest of
           frocks,
And Bertie should chance to look in at
           our box:
(He's tall and extravagant, well-dressed
           and *dear* –
A poor younger son, who has nothing a
           year!)
I know why he comes, for he's bored
           with the play,
I see, by his eyes, what he's longing to
           say –
Though forced to reply in my frigidest
           tone,
I wish I could *strangle* my stiff
           chaperon!

What, from the point of view of the girl's chaperon – and her parents – was wrong with Bertie?

Getting Married

It was difficult for a single woman to earn enough to support herself: girls were brought up to believe that their natural "career" was marriage to a man who could provide a home for his wife and family. Unmarried women were pitied (though Charles Dickens in his story *David Copperfield* described a very jolly, happy spinster called Betsy Trotwood. She had money of her own, however).

SUPERSTITIONS

There were lucky and unlucky colours for a wedding dress (green was very unlucky). A rhyme in Oxfordshire went . . .

> Married in black, you'll wish you were back,
> Married in green, not fit to be seen,
> Married in brown, you'll never live in a town.

Do you know of any superstitions about weddings today?

FINDING A HUSBAND

Rich girls were carefully introduced to suitable young men and taken to dances by their mothers. Village girls from poor families had to take advantage of any contacts they could make. Flora Thompson described the courtships and marriages of her friends in her Oxfordshire village in the 1880s and 1890s:

> A few of the girls were engaged to youths at home, and, after several years of courtship, mostly conducted by letter, for they seldom met except during the girl's summer holiday [from domestic service], they would marry and settle in or near the hamlet. Others married and settled away. Butchers and milkmen were favoured as husbands, perhaps because these were frequent callers at the houses where the girls were employed ... One married a butler ... (*Lark Rise to Candleford*, 1939)

WEDDING CUSTOMS IN A COUNTRY TOWN

The writer Elizabeth Gaskell told a friend in a letter about the way the people of Knutsford in Cheshire in the 1830s decorated the ground in front of their houses when a wedding took place,

> ... strewing the ground ... with common red sand, and then taking a funnel filled with white sand, and sprinkling a pattern of flowers upon the red ground. This is always done for a wedding, and often accompanied by some verse .... When I was married, nearly all the houses in the town were sanded and these were the two favourite verses:

> Long may they live
> Happy may they be,
> Blest with content,
> And from misfortune free.

> Long may they live,
> Happy may they be,
> And blest with a numerous
> Pro /ge /ny

(Quoted in Winifred Gerin, *Elizabeth Gaskell*, 1976)

Can you guess what "progeny" means? (Check your guess on p. 44).

A RICH GIRL GETS ENGAGED

Mary Gladstone, daughter of a famous politician who later became Prime Minister, described in her diary the excitement of her cousin's preparations for marriage:

1864
London, April 21. After breakfast, Lucy's engagement [to Lord Frederick Cavendish] finally settled in the conservatory and given out to the household . . .
London, April 25. Mama began to buy her trousseau. Her wedding lace was bought . . .
London, April 30. Went shopping for Lucy's trousseau. Got eight silk gowns, two muslin, shawl, etc. Great fun! (*Mary Gladstone, Diaries and Letters*, ed. Lucy Masterman, 1930)

Do you know, or can you work out, what a "trousseau" was? Have you ever heard the word used today? Mrs Gladstone was buying Lucy's trousseau because Lucy's mother was dead.

WEDDING DRESSES

Though rich girls had elaborate dresses, girls from poor families wore their best dress, or if they could afford a new one they chose something that would wear well for years to come. Such a dress was not likely to be white.

She was dressed in grey with dashes of brightness, and under a little hat her dark hair was coiled magnificently. Her jacket . . . was of finest serge, fitting closely at the waist . . . the shaped cuffs were bordered with cherry-red velvet ribbon . . . . Her hat had a high crown and a small brim with a bunch of cherries and grey ribbon at the front.
(M.K. Ashby, *Joseph Ashby of Tysoe*, 1961)

Kathleen Ashby heard these details of her mother's wedding clothes when she was a child. Hannah, the bride, was married to a labourer just beginning to move up in the world. Find the "dashes of brightness" in the wedding outfit.

Queen Victoria's wedding dress was made of white satin and lace. She married Prince Albert in February 1840, in St James's Palace Chapel, in London.

Having Children

Families were usually large in nineteenth-century Britain. There was little knowledge of family planning, and women of all social groups sometimes had more babies than was good for their health. Having a baby was dangerous then, too, and young women knew that if anything went wrong they might die: doctors did not know how to prevent or cure any problems in the way they do today. Once safely born, young children were also much more at risk than they now are, and many mothers faced the sorrow of a child's death.

The death of a baby was a common tragedy in the nineteenth century. Here the artist shows a mother dressed in black, sitting beside an empty cradle. The picture (1873) is called "The Mother's First Grief": everyone who saw it would know what was meant.
▼

MRS BEETON'S ADVICE TO MOTHERS

Although women were expected to marry and have children it was not expected that rich women would look after the children themselves. Mrs Beeton, writing for the comfortably off, urged mothers to keep in closer contact with their young families.

A mother's responsibilities are the greatest that a woman can have .... No matter what good nurses and attendants she may be able to engage for her little ones, what pleasures, changes of air, model nurseries, toys and books she may afford for their benefit, she should still devote *some* part of her time to them at any rate ....

The children's hour should be an institution in every household .... Let praise be given for little tasks well done, disputes be settled ... and let a game or tale ... conclude the happy hour. Should this, as it often happens, be just the time generally given to afternoon tea, let the little ones bring this to their mother and wait upon her as children love to do. She will not find an hour wasted in this way, even if it be one hard to spare. (*Household Management*, 1861)

Who would look after children from this kind of family for the rest of the day (and night)? You will find more about this on p. 18.

These three girls from an ordinary Welsh family ▶ were photographed around 1890. Older sisters were expected to help look after younger children: do you think the photographer has been able to suggest this in the photograph?

TRAINING FUTURE MOTHERS

Elizabeth Gaskell, a writer who was married to a clergyman, had enough money to pay for help with her children. Even so, she gave a great deal of her time to her family and carefully supervised her daughters' education (she had a baby son, too, as you can see from the extract, but he died of scarlet fever at ten months). She described the daily routine in one of her letters:

½ past 5 Margaret [nursemaid] brings Florence's supper, which Marianne gives her ... while Meta goes up stairs to get ready and fold up Willie's basket of clothes while he is undressed (this by way of feminine and family duties) ...
(Letter, 1845, quoted in *Elizabeth Gaskell* by Winifred Gerin, 1976)

The two eldest girls, Marianne and Meta, were aged 11 and 8 at this time. Are you expected to help look after your younger brothers and sisters at home?

POVERTY BRINGS TRAGEDY

Life was very different for mothers trying to keep large families alive on low incomes. One Oxfordshire woman was overwhelmed by her situation, with tragic results.

The Oxford Times, 16 January, 1886
Infanticide: On Saturday, much excitement was caused in the usually quiet village of Tiddington, near Thame, by the report ... that Mrs Nelms, the wife of Cook Nelms, a ganger on the Great Western Railway, had murdered her infant child .... The mother sat in a chair in a corner of the room, in an apparently dazed condition, and seemingly unconscious of what was going on .... The helpless little victim was the youngest of a family of twelve, nine of whom are living, and the mother, up to within the last three weeks, has been an industrious, hard-working woman, fond of her children, an affectionate wife, and kind and pleasant to her friends and relatives.

Latterly, however, there has been some trouble in the home, owing to two of the sons being out of work, and the poor mother appears to have had great difficulty in obtaining sufficient food for her numerous family. This seems to have preyed upon her mind .... The unfortunate child was about five months old ...

What reasons for this mother's breakdown can you find in this account?

Running a Household

When there were several children and a number of servants to supervise, a wife had to take care that everything ran smoothly (most nineteenth-century husbands did not expect to be bothered about household matters). In poor families there was much hard work to be done by the mother if everyone was to be clean, respectably dressed and properly fed.

WASHDAY

With few labour-saving devices and no detergents to remove dirt, washday was a major concern for the housewife. Mrs Beeton advised her readers on how to be really well organized:

A good laundry establishment for a large household consists of a washing-house, an ironing and drying-room, and sometimes a drying-closet heated by furnaces. The washing-house will probably be attached to the kitchen; but it is better that it should be completely detached from it . . . with a funnel . . . to carry off the steam . . . . The contents of [the drying-room] should comprise an ironing-board, opposite to the light; a strong white deal table . . . a mangle in one corner, and clothes-horses for drying and airing; cupboards for holding the various irons, starch, and other articles used in ironing; a hot-plate built in the chimney, with furnace beneath it for heating the irons . . . (*Household Management*, 1861)

(Mrs Beeton then goes on to list the various stages of the wash – Soaking, Washing, Boiling, Mangling, Starching and Ironing are all included).

Even quite small houses had wash-houses attached: you may have some examples in your area. Imagine, though, what washday was like for

HOUSEHOLD HINTS

Many magazines included hints for housewives. This helpful advice comes from a church magazine and is a reminder of how many things ordinary mothers had to do that they don't have to bother with today.

The Housewife's Corner
Boots – Housewives may save themselves much trouble and anxious care, and their children many coughs and colds, if they pay close attention to the boots of the family . . . . See to it that the old boots are double-soled, to resist the rain and snow of winter. When you know your children will have to trudge through thick snow, or when heavy rain threatens, try greasing the leather with mutton fat or common yellow soap; either will do much to keep out the wet. When the bairns come home, see to it that the boots come off at once, and if they are soaked through, stuff them as tightly as possible with hay or straw. (*Home Words for Heart and Hearth*, 1898)

Girls as well as boys wore boots, as you can see, on p. 00. What were these boots made of? What are wet-weather boots made of today to make them waterproof?

poorer families without separate washing or drying rooms.

Make a list of the equipment in your house for washing and ironing the family's clothes, sheets and towels. How are they dried? How many of your own clothes need to be ironed?

COOKING

Cooking was an important skill for all except the richest women. Even housewives who kept several servants would cook special delicacies, Miss C.W. Pumphrey remembered her Quaker relations in Charlbury, Oxfordshire, in the mid-nineteenth century taking pride in their baking:

Each house had its speciality . . . .

CLEAN HOUSES IN MANCHESTER

Though married women in Lancashire often worked in the textile factories – the mills – they could still pride themselves on their well-kept houses.

Saturday is generally the great weekly epoch of cleansing and setting things to rights in the homes of the Manchester workpeople . . . . The mills knock off work at about two or half after two o'clock . . . . The women, of course, are the principal operators – they are cleaning their windows, hearthstoning their lintels [white stones over doors or windows], scrubbing their furniture with might and main. The *pater familias* [father of the family] however does not always shirk his portion of the toil. Only last Saturday I came upon two or three lords of the creation usefully employed in blackleading their stoves. (A Morning Chronicle reporter's letter from Manchester, 1849-50, quoted in *Selections from Letters to the Morning Chronicle*, ed. Razzell and Wainwright, 1973)

Why did these women clean their houses on Saturday afternoon?

Grandmamma, as a Somersetshire woman, excelled in junket and buttermilk bread. Aunt Carry shone in gingerbread nuts and, after the invention of baking powder, in what she called 'head-cakes' . . . . Aunt Hannah instituted a good substantial bun. There were no confectioners in Charlbury then, and no baker ever got nearer it than a hot cross bun, a thing not allowed in good Quaker households. (Ms., Oxford City Library)

What difference did baking powder make to cakes? (Ask an older friend or relation if you don't know.) Can you find out why hot cross buns were not allowed in good Quaker households?

This Punch *cartoon is making a point against working men who were campaigning in 1871 for a shorter working day. Which things in the picture show what kept their wives busy for long hours in the home?*

"SAUCE FOR THE GANDER."

"I SAY, JOE, DEAR. IF YOU CAN'T ENJOY YOUR SUPPER NOW YOU HAVE LOST YOUR GRUMBLE ABOUT NINE HOURS—GRUMBLE FOR ME, AS I'VE DONE FOURTEEN, AND AIN'T FINISHED YET."

Making Ends Meet

In poor families a wife's earnings, however small, could make the difference between survival and starvation. The poor resorted to all kinds of measures to raise a little extra money. Pawning goods (that is, raising loans on them, with the risk of losing the articles if the money could not be repaid) was the most common way of tiding over hard times.

ECONOMIZING ON FOOD

Late in the nineteenth century Charles Booth investigated poverty in London. He found many women struggling to keep going on very little money.

> No. 1 – This is the poorest case on my list .... The neighbouring clergy send soup 2 or 3 times a week, and practically no meat is bought ... the food consists principally of bread, margarine, tea and sugar ... there is no sign of any but the most primitive cookery, but there is every sign of unshrinking economy ... the prices are the lowest possible .... Allowing as well as I can for the meals out [dinners for the father and son when they were working], and the charitable soup, I make the meals provided by Mrs H— for her family to cost 1d. per meal per person (counting the two little girls as one person) ....
> (Charles Booth, *Life and Labour of the People in London*, 1889-1902)

This family let two of their four rooms to make a little extra money, and to add to Mrs "H"'s troubles, she was "consumptive", that is, she had tuberculosis, a very dangerous disease at this time.

Look again at this family's diet: in what ways is it inadequate?

HELP FROM A SON

Young people often helped their parents with money, especially if the mother was a widow. William Lanceley, a 16-year-old in domestic service in 1870, took his first year's salary of £8 home

> ... handing it over with pride to my mother. She had been left a widow with nine children, the eldest eighteen years of age, and to make matters worse my father had died in debt. I can still see her face when she took it and then, giving me £2 back, said 'I cannot take it all, lad.'
> 'But, Mother', I pleaded, 'you must want it and I can get plenty in tips to keep me.'
> On leaving I put the £2 quietly on the cottage table where I knew she would find it .... (William Lanceley, *From Hall-Boy to House-Steward*, 1925 quoted in *Useful Toil*, ed. John Burnett, 1974)

A London street-seller at the end of the nineteenth century.

GETTING THROUGH BAD TIMES

Henry Mayhew, a journalist, met many of the London poor in the 1840s and recorded their life histories. His articles were republished as a book, *London Labour and the London Poor*, in 1861-2. One middle-aged married woman had this story to tell:

> About seven years ago we were very badly off – no work, and no money, and neither of us well. . . . So at last . . . my gold wedding-ring that cost 8s. 6d., and that I'd stuck to all along, had to be pawned for 4s. 6d. for rent and bread. That *was* a shocking time, sir . . . .
>
> All this time I could do nothing – though I tried for washing and charing, but I'm slow at washing – but starve at home, and be afraid every knock was the landlord. After that John [her husband] was employed to carry a very heavy board over his shoulder, and so as to have it read on both sides. It was about an eating-house, and I went with him to give little bills about it to all we met . . . . He had 1s. a day, and I had 6d. That was my first time in the streets and I felt so 'shamed to come to that . . . .

For once, the story had a happy ending, as eventually this couple got a little money given to them and were able to do quite well as street-sellers.

The following extract was from an interview with a young woman in her twenties:

> I used to mind my mother's stall . . . when I was a girl . . . . Mother's been dead these – well I don't know how long, but it's a long time. I've lived by myself ever since, and kept myself, and I have half a room with another young woman who lives by making little boxes . . . . We pays 1s. 6d. a-week between us; it's my bed, and the other sticks [furniture] is her'n. We 'gree well enough . . . . I've sold small wares in the streets, and artificials [artificial flowers], and lace, and penny dolls, and penny boxes [of toys] . . . . I'm a-going to leave the streets. I have an aunt a laundress . . . and she taught me laundressing. I work for her three and sometimes four days a week now . . . .

How was this woman keeping her living costs down? How many different ways for poor women to earn money can you find in this account?

Women who took in laundry work, like this character from Charles Dickens' story The Old Curiosity Shop, *worked late at night in cramped conditions. Notice the flat-irons (which had to be heated on the fire). What were the big baskets used for?*
▼

Women and the Workhouse

After 1834, poor people needing help from the Poor Rate – the tax paid to keep people from actually starving – had to go into a workhouse if they were fit to work. Women often needed help because they were single parents or widows with children. In the workhouse they were separated from their children (and married couples were also separated from each other).

A MOTHER'S FEELINGS

Henry Mayhew heard this sad story from a widow in London in 1849:

> Between ten and eleven years ago I was left a widow . . . . I got so little [from shirt-making] that I found it impossible to live . . . never shall I forget that Saturday afternoon, as I travelled along Gravel-lane [in Wapping] to the "house", with feelings that it was impossible for me to enter, for I thought "How can I bear to have my dear children taken away from me – they have never been taken away from me before." I reflected, "What can I do but go there?" . . . I was admitted to a room where they were toasting the bread for the mistress's tea. A little girl was there, and she said, "Look at those dear little children, I will give them a bit of the toast." The children took it, and thought it very nice, but they little thought that we were so soon to be parted. The first was seven years old, the second, three, and the infant was in my arms. A mother's feelings are better felt than described. The children were taken and separated . . . (Henry Mayhew, *The Morning Chronicle Survey of Labour and the Poor: The Metropolitan Districts*, Vol. 1, republished 1980)

Though in this workhouse both the master and the mistress were kind and tried to help, one of these children died of measles before the mother could get the family out and back together again.

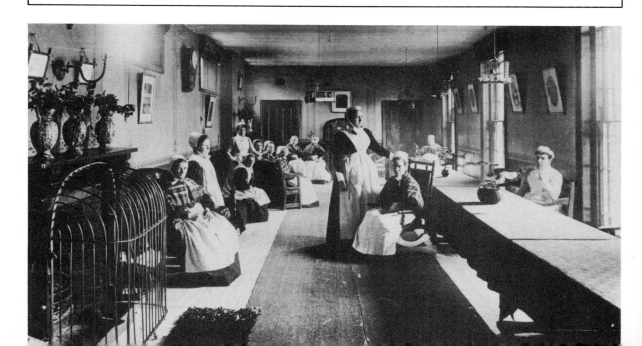

GIRLS FROM THE WORKHOUSE

When pauper girls were old enough to work for a living they were placed in jobs. These were almost always in domestic service. Sometimes, though, there was a feeling that a girl might do better than this.

Bromley Union Ladies' Committee Visitors' Reports, 1897
Eva Graham, aged 13, living in Wellington Road is very high up in School – in the 7th Standard. She is quick and unusually intelligent and Mrs Williams, our Visitor, is anxious to know if the guardians would be willing to allow her to become a pupil teacher. This would necessitate her remaining somewhat longer than usual on our list, but it seems to be a most suitable opening for the girl.

Sadly, the enterprising Mrs Williams did not have her way: the next report records,

... as the foster-home is rather a poor one, and the girl is not overstrong, it would be wise to let her go to service....

Notice that, like many other places at this date, Bromley has a Ladies' Committee, made up of local ladies ready to take an interest in the poor and their treatment. At first, only men could be elected as Guardians (the people who supervised the relief of the poor in each area after 1834). After 1875 women, too, were allowed to stand for election, but few were actually elected.

The women's ward of Wolverhampton workhouse, 1900. Can you pick out the paid members of staff in their smart uniforms?

RUNNING THE WORKHOUSE

In the first part of the nineteenth century only pauper women (that is, people helped from the Poor Rate) were used as nurses, and sometimes as teachers too, in the workhouses. Later, more women were employed from outside to do a wide range of jobs, as you can see from the list below.

Annual Report of the Guardians of the Poor, Oxford
1874-5
Workhouse officers

Master Mr E.C. Stedham	£80.0.0
Matron Mrs Stedham	£40.0.0
Porter John Turner	£20.0.0
Tramp Attendant E. Turner	£10.0.0
Nurse Mary Dickens	£30.0.0
Assistant Nurse Elizabeth Garrod	£20.0.0
Pantry Woman Catherine Trotman	£18.0.0
Labour Master Thomas Simmonds	£20.00
Barber James White	£15.0.0
Superintendent and Schoolmaster Mr Edmund Kerby	£40.0.0
(plus a share of the government grant)	
Sewing Mistress and Schoolmistress Mrs Kerby	£20
Gardener and Porter I. Redwood	15s a week
Cook Charlotte Payne	£16.0.0
Laundress Elizabeth Wise	£16.0.0

Which woman worker is the best paid? And the second-best? What do you notice about the matron and the schoolmistress? What subject being taught to women and girls in the workhouse is obviously thought important?

Though the chief nurses in this workhouse infirmary were trained and paid they would still have been helped by untrained paupers.

In Service

"Going into service" was the normal way of earning a living for many girls. In large houses there were opportunities for promotion and a woman could make a good living as cook or housekeeper. The maid-of-all-work, or general servant, in a less prosperous home was often over-worked, badly paid and very lonely.

WORK IN A COUNTRY HOUSE

After a year's training in a local job — with a tradesman's or school-teacher's family perhaps — girls from Flora Thompson's Oxfordshire village tried to get living-in places with wealthy families. Girls usually took their first jobs at around 12. They began at the bottom, but hoped to work their way up to better positions in the servants' hall of the big houses.

> **The girls who "went into the kitchen" began as scullery maids, washing up stacks of dishes, cleaning saucepans and dish covers, preparing vegetables, and doing the kitchen scrubbing and other rough work. After a year or two of this, they became under kitchen maids and worked up gradually until they were second in command to the cook. When they reached that point, they did much of the actual cooking . . . .**
>
> **Some girls preferred house to kitchen work, and they would be found a place in some mansion as third or fourth house-maid and work upward . . . . The under servants in big houses began at seven pounds a year, which was increased at each advancement, until, as head house-maid, they might receive as much as thirty. A good cook could ask fifty, and even obtain another five by threatening to leave . . . .** (*Lark Rise to Candleford*, published 1939-45, but recording conditions in the 1880s and 1890s)

NURSES AND NURSEMAIDS

A family nurse was often a very important person to the children; sometimes she stayed on long after the children grew up. Marianne Thornton wrote about her nurse, Nurse Hunter (who died in about 1850, after 52 years with the family):

> **I have never once seen her worried or put out unless when she found the children were hurting themselves, she was constantly at hand . . . & knew all that went on, & gave me as good advice about the servants as she could have done 10 years ago. There is nobody to whom I could, & did, tell everything as I did to her, & there was no one who could give me such good advice.** (Quoted in E.M. Forster, *Marianne Thornton*, 1956)

In big houses, nursemaids assisted the nurse.

> **The under nursemaid lights the fires, sweeps, scours and dusts the rooms, and makes the beds, empties slops and carries up water, brings up and removes the nursery meals, washes and dresses all the children, except the infant [the baby] and assists in mending.** (Mrs Beeton, *Household Management*, 1861)

Census figures for 1871 show that 51 per cent of nursemaids were under 20, and 23 per cent were under 14. How attractive a job would this be to a young girl?

There were many restrictions imposed on servants, though: many had no fixed time off and had to ask permission if they wanted to go somewhere. You can find out how they had to dress on p. 39.

A MAID'S WAGES

May 17. Susan Baker comes; her wages 8 pound a year.
July 17. Gave Susan one pound on account of wages.
August 17. Paid Susan one pound the remainder of her quarter's wages.
(Diary of Mary Anne Marshall Hacker, 1854, Oxfordshire County Archives)

How often was Susan paid when she did not need to ask for some money in advance? (Perhaps she needed to send money home. Flora Thompson knew village girls who paid rent or coal bills for their parents.)

SERVANTS WANTED

Newspaper advertisements give useful information about domestic service. How much can you learn from these advertisements?

General servant wanted for London suburbs. Comfortable home, wages £10; age 17-20

House parlourmaid required, early next month. Country girl, clean and good-tempered. No fringe. Churchwoman. Apply by letter only to Mrs T, 6, Keble Road, Oxford.
(*Jackson's Oxford Journal*, January 1898)

This Punch *cartoon (1888) shows how much control a mistress expected to have over a servant: maids were not supposed to have male visitors unless they were relations.*

Judging from the evidence on these pages, if you had to go into service in the nineteenth century, which kind of job would you have preferred? Which would you have liked least?

"THE FLATTERING TALE."

Old Lady ("*down upon Followers*"). "THAT YOUNG MAN WHO IS JUST GOING OUT, I SUPPOSE, IS YOUR BROTHER, JANE?"
Maid. "NO, 'M. NOT MY BROTHER, M'UM,—WHICH HE'S A YOUNG MAN, M'UM,—MOST R'SPECT'BLE, M'UM,—AS I'VE 'OPES OF!!"

Factory Girls

During the nineteenth century more women found jobs outside the home, some of them in the factories set up as part of Britain's industrial revolution. As you will see, these jobs brought both advantages and disadvantages for women. Though working conditions were bad at first for both men and women, improvements were made during the century (you will find it interesting to discover for yourselves about these factory reforms).

You can see from this Union Card which group of women factory workers had a union of their own in the 1830s. In Lancashire, men and women cotton weavers belonged to the same union, but women were expected to take a back seat. In 1877 Mr Birtwhistle of the Accrington cotton weavers explained that in his union, "the women [9000] rather outnumbered the men, but the business was principally conducted by men. They always found the women willing to assist, and very ready and regular in their payments."

The Bearer

Ellen Reily

Has been admitted a Member of the
WEST OF SCOTLAND
Power Loom Female Weavers Society

Glasgow 22 March 1833   No 5701

PROFITABLE EMPLOYMENT IN LANCASHIRE

Textile factories employed many women and girls to work spinning machines and power looms (which wove the cloth). In 1851 there were 255,000 men and 272,000 women cotton workers. Though hours of work were long, wages were comparatively high, and women could even earn as much as the men.

> **... in Lancashire profitable employment for females is abundant. Domestic servants are in consequence so scarce that they can only be obtained from the neighbouring counties.**
>
> **A young woman, prudent and careful, and living with her parents, from the age of 16 to 25, may, in that time, by factory employment, save £100 as a wedding portion .... She is not then driven into an early marriage by the necessity of seeking a home ....** ("Hand-loom Weavers' Report, 1840", quoted in Royston Pike, ed., *Human Documents of the Industrial Revolution*, 1966)

Why were domestic servants scarce in Lancashire?

A LANCASHIRE SONG, 1810

See if you can work out from this verse one thing that made factory work less pleasant than working at home.

> **So come all you cotton-weavers,**
>   **You must rise up very soon**
> **For you must work in factories**
>   **From morning until noon:**
> **You mustn't walk in your garden**
>   **For two or three hours a day**
> **For you must stand at their command,**
>   **And keep your shuttles in play.**
> ("Song of 1810", quoted in Dave Harker, *One for the Money*, 1980)

THE PLEASURES OF INDEPENDENCE

Walter Besant, who studied London and its history, wrote an interesting description of the life of London factory girls in the 1880s.

There is . . . below the shop-girls, the dressmakers, the servants, and the working girls whom the world, so to speak, knows, a very large class of women whom the world does not know, and is not anxious to know. They are the factory hands of London; you can see them, if you wish, trooping out of the factories and places where they work on any Saturday afternoon . . . . Their amusement seems to consist of nothing but walking about the streets, two and three abreast, and they laugh and shout as they go so noisily that they must needs be extraordinarily happy. These girls are, I am told, for the most part so ignorant and helpless, that many of them do not know even how to use a needle; they cannot read, or, if they can, they never do; they carry the virtue of independence as far as they are able, and insist on living by themselves, two sharing a single room; nor will they brook [put up with] the least interference with their freedom, even from those who try to help them . . . . Their pay is said to be wretched, whatever work they do; their food . . . is insufficient for young and hearty girls, consisting generally of tea and bread or bread-and-butter for breakfast and supper, and for dinner a lump of fried fish and a piece of bread . . . (Walter Besant, "The Amusements of the People", *Contemporary Review*, 1884)

WORKING MOTHERS

Married women working in a factory had special problems once they started a family. At home they might have to work long hours but at least they had their young children with them. Here a journalist reports on child-minding in Oldham in 1849:

Presently I overtook two little girls, the eldest not above eight years of age, each carrying a baby some three or four months old . . . I accosted [spoke to] them.
"So you have these children to nurse? What do the mothers pay you?"
"Oh, please sir, they pay us one shilling and sixpence a week for each baby."
"And where are you taking them now?"
"Oh, please sir, to their mothers. They come out of the mills now, and we carry the babies down to meet them, and the mothers give them suck [breast-feed them] when they're at dinner" . . . . (P.E. Razzell and R.W. Wainwright, eds., *The Victorian Working Class, Selections from Letters to the Morning Chronicle*, 1973)

Would mothers today be prepared to have their babies in the care of such young children?

You will notice that, unlike the Lancashire weavers, these factory workers are not well paid. Compare the London factory girls' life with life in domestic service (pp. 18-19). Make up a discussion between a Victorian father and his daughter; she wants to take work in a factory, he wants her to go into service. Try to find really good arguments on both sides.

Sweated Labour

Workers who were paid low rates for the completed articles they produced, either at home or in small workshops, were called "sweated workers": they had to work very long hours to make enough to live on. Many, though not all, of these workers were women.

GLOVE-MAKING

Women married to low-paid workers such as farm labourers often did work at home to make a little extra money. You can see from the following description how this work was organized.

> The material is sent in the piece from London to the agent in some central place in Somersetshire, Devonshire, Worcestershire, as the case may be. On his premises a few men are employed to cut out, and then the various parts of the glove are given out to be sewn together. The people who do that are wives and daughters of agricultural labourers . . . . If they live near they bring in their work as it is finished; if far off, probably someone goes round once a fortnight and collects all that is ready, bringing it in for a small percentage . . . . ("Report of Royal Commission on Children's Employment, 1864", quoted in Duncan Bythell, *The Sweated Trades*, 1978)

Can you think of any reasons why this type of worker would be willing to accept low wages?

◀ Punch *campaigned against sweated labour: this mock advertisement appeared in May 1888. Do you think it would have made prospective customers think twice about where their fine clothes came from?*

This illustration from The Sunday Magazine *(1869) shows the living quarters of a family of sweated workers. How much light have the girls to sew by? What heating and cooking facilities are there? What is the sick boy's bed made from, and why is it put in that particular place? Notice the roll of material on the chest. The story explains that this is heavy, oily cloth, which smells so badly that the window has to be open despite the cold.*
▼

DRESSMAKING

In the towns most dressmaking was done by home workers or in small workshops, which were often so overcrowded that they were unhealthy. Charles Dickens claimed that it was always easy to recognize London girls who worked in these "sweatshops":

> ... the pale face with its hectic bloom [flush], the slight distortion of form which no artifice [trick] of dress can wholly conceal, the unhealthy stoop, and the short cough – the effects of hard work and close application to sedentary employment [work done while sitting down] ...
>
> (Charles Dickens, *Reprinted Pieces*, 1858)

(The flushed cheeks and cough were signs of tuberculosis.)

A great problem for dressmakers was the sudden demand by customers for new clothes in a hurry. This could happen when mourning was needed if a relative died, or if there was a big occasion like a "Drawing-Room", or special party, at the Palace. The writer Thomas Hood described the working day of girls at a fashionable dressmaker's in 1860:

> Out of bed and to work at six or half-past. A coarse breakfast at eight, then work again until a one o'clock dinner. After that work until a scanty tea, followed by more work until supper at nine, and from that hour till twelve once more work! This is the ordinary work-day, but when a Drawing Room or any great occasion is at hand they have frequently to work all night.
>
> (Thomas Hood, *Living and Dying by the Needle*, 1860)

Thomas Hood also wrote a famous poem called "Song of the Shirt" about home workers. Ask your public library if they have a copy of Hood's poems.

A WOMAN SHOE-BINDER

In 1849, Henry Mayhew collected information from many sweated workers in Victorian London. One of them told him,

> I make snow boots at present. I bind them ... the cloth and lining is cut out and given out by the warehouse. We have to stitch them together, make the button-holes, and sew on the binding and the buttons. I get seven farthings per pair and find [pay for] my own thread and cotton. That costs about a halfpenny [2 farthings] per pair .... It takes about three hours and a half to do one pair. We can't earn more than two shillings a week at our work. A person must work very hard to do three pair a day, but it's impossible to do that every day .... I'm up by six, and don't leave off till twelve or one, and then I can't do more than three pair. It takes twelve hours' continual work to do three pair. The rest of the time I must mind my children .... (Henry Mayhew, *The Morning Chronicle Survey of Labour and the Poor: The Metropolitan Districts*, Vol. I, 1849; reprinted 1980)

Low pay for women sewing in their own homes is still a problem today: an article in the *Guardian* in 1986 quoted wages for Leicester home workers as low as 50p an hour. You may be able to find other newspaper or magazine articles on this subject.

Use the material on this page to make up a story about the life of a sweated worker in the middle of the nineteenth century.

Governesses

Well into the second half of the nineteenth century the only paid employment considered suitable for a young lady was private teaching, usually as governess in a wealthy family. Pay was generally low (though a very well educated governess might earn £100 p.a. the average was £20-£45), and elderly, retired governesses had no pensions.

IN NEED OF A SITUATION

Charlotte Brontë was the daughter of a Church of England clergyman: she was, therefore, a lady. However, her father was poor, and his daughters needed to earn their living. Charlotte wrote a joking letter to a friend in which she pretended that she might take an unsuitable job, instead of the only possible one – that of governess.

> 15 April 1839
> For my own part, I am yet "wanting a situation", like a housemaid out of a place. By the way, I have lately discovered I have quite a talent for cleaning, sweeping up hearths, dusting rooms, making beds, etc; so if everything else fails, I can turn my hand to that, if anybody will give me good wages for little labour. I won't be a cook; I hate cooking. I won't be a nursery maid, nor a lady's maid, far less a lady's companion, or a mantua-maker [coat-maker], or a straw-bonnet maker, or a taker-in of plain work [sewing]. I won't be anything but a house-maid ...
> (Quoted in Elizabeth Gaskell, *Life of Charlotte Brontë*, 1857)

Within a few weeks, Charlotte was acting as governess to a rich family where, she complained bitterly, the children were "to do as they like", and where her employer was only interested in trying to get as much work as possible out of her – "she overwhelms me with oceans of needlework". Later, Charlotte Brontë wrote a famous novel about a governess. Do you know, or can you find out, what it is called?

Can you find anyone in this picture of people waiting to emigrate who looks as if she might be a governess?

A FRIEND AND COMPANION

Sometimes a governess could form a happy relationship with her pupil or pupils. Jane Austen, in her novel *Emma* (published in 1816), wrote about her heroine's sorrow when her governess left to get married:

> **Sixteen years had Miss Taylor been in Mr Woodhouse's family, less as a governess than a friend, very fond of both daughters, but particularly of Emma. Between them it was more the intimacy of sisters . . . . She had been a friend and companion such as few possessed: intelligent, well-informed, useful, gentle, knowing all the ways of the family, interested in all its concerns.**

Emma's mother had died before Miss Taylor arrived: what difference would this make to the governess's position?

It was not only in fiction that governesses had happy relationships with their pupils: the Capel family, mentioned on p. 7, persuaded their Miss Jones to follow them to Europe in 1814, bringing her elderly father with her.

A WARNING TO PARENTS

The governess's position was an awkward one, as she was neither a servant nor an equal of the family that employed her. The author and artist John Ruskin criticized employers for their attitude towards their governesses.

> **What reverence do you show to the teachers you have chosen? Is a girl likely to think her own conduct, or her own intellect, of much importance, when you trust the entire formation of her character . . . to a person whom you let your servants treat with less respect**

GOVERNESSES ABROAD

Perhaps not surprisingly, some women felt that they would do better as governesses in the British colonies overseas. A society called the Female Middle Class Emigration Society lent money to those wishing to try their luck in Australia. Some, though not all, of the emigrants did well. Read the following extracts from letters written back to the Society, and you will be able to pick out at least two different opportunities offered by Australia to the women who went.

Letter from Miss Barlow, 1863 (she set up a small school near Melbourne):

> **I am getting quite a Colonial Woman, and fear I should not easily fit into English ideas again – can scrub a floor with anyone, and bake my own bread and many other things an English governess and Schoolmistress would be horrified at . . . . I have great hopes of [my] sister succeeding here in photography.**

Letter from Mrs White, 1881:

> **Pretty, lady-like girls who go on distant stations [farms] are certain to marry well. The Australian men seem to have quite a fancy for marrying governesses, and it is not at all usual to look for money with a wife . . . .** (Quoted in Patricia Clarke, *The Governesses*, 1985)

Do you think you would have preferred being a governess in England or in Australia?

> **than they do your housekeeper . . . and whom you yourself think you confer an honour upon by letting her sometimes sit in the drawing room in the evening.** (John Ruskin, *Sesame and Lilies*, 1865)

Elementary Schoolteachers

As nineteenth-century education reforms led to more schools being built, school-teaching developed as a career for women as well as for men. Clever girls from poor families were able to act as monitors, helping teachers with the younger children. From the 1840s onwards they could train as pupil-teachers, some of them going on to study at teacher-training colleges. Girls like these taught in elementary schools, which provided elementary (simple) education for poor children.

THE SCHOOLTEACHER'S STATUS

For a girl from a poor family a teaching job was an improvement on other kinds of work available, such as domestic service or even serving in a shop. However, elementary schoolteachers were still low on the social scale. An article of 1873 discussed whether or not a lady could even consider becoming one:

Stockwell College, shown here in 1874, was opened in London in 1861 for women students. The students practised their teaching in the school on the right of the picture.

Ladies cannot, it may be said, become mistresses of elementary schools without ceasing to be ladies. They may conceivably be reduced to this in order to save themselves from starvation, just as they may be reduced for the same reason to go out as domestic servants .... (*Cornhill Magazine*, Vol. 28, 1873)

The author of the article argued that despite the possible loss of social status a lady would be better off becoming a schoolmistress than going as a governess to a family, for she would "have Saturdays and Sundays to herself".

THE TRIALS OF A VILLAGE SCHOOLMISTRESS

The Church of England school in Little Faringdon, Oxfordshire, had about 25 children attending in the 1890s. There was only one schoolmistress and, although 25 sounds quite a reasonable size for a class even today, the children varied in age from four to 13. Catharine Wright Shepperd, certificated teacher of the Second class, seems from the Inspectors' reports to have been bad at her job. However, she herself reported many problems in the school log-book:

1891
April 10. The want of a Monitor to help look after the Infants is felt throughout the School, the Mistress having with them all Standards [classes] to teach. April 23. The constant presence of a child of 9 years who cannot learn and requires individual management hinders progress of others. (*Little Faringdon School Log-Book*, 1879-1900)

After a series of bad reports from Inspectors, "Miss

SUITABLE SCHOOLTEACHERS

The following letter praising the training given at Whitelands (a Church of England training college) shows what was generally expected of a teacher in a small village school:

The system of training there seems to me perfect and they make a very great point of needlework, particularly cutting out, and shirt-making and gown-making as well as fine work [embroidery]. There seems such a desire to make them really humble unpretending Village Teachers, making them clean and cook and iron (not wash) that they mayn't fancy themselves fine ladies *because* they teach them Geography & History and so on. (Letter of the 1850s from Marianne Thornton, quoted in E.M. Forster, *Marianne Thornton*, 1956)

Marianne Thornton was a rich lady. Why would she be pleased that the Whitelands' girls should be made to feel humble? Today Whitelands is part of Roehampton Institute of Higher Education. You may find their prospectus in your local library. Try to discover what students training to teach are able to study today.

Shepperd gave up the school" when she departed for her summer holidays in 1893.

One advantage of being a schoolmistress in charge of a school was that a house was usually provided rent-free. The house at Little Faringdon lacked its own water-supply however. An Inspector reported in May 1898 that "all the water used in the school and the teacher's house has to be brought a distance of about 300 yards". Even when this situation improved, the improvement consisted of digging a school well!

=====Caring for the Sick=====

"It is in times of sickness that a woman's work and worth are seen to the best advantage", wrote Frank Mundell in a book meant to inspire girls of the late nineteenth century, *Heroines of Mercy*. Women looked after the old and the sick in their own families (as many still do). During the nineteenth century, though, nursing also became a profession for women, and a few women even managed to train as doctors.

Mrs Beeton automatically assumed that women needed advice on home nursing. In this early twentieth-century edition of Household Management, *though, the editor also assumed that trained nurses were available to help those who could afford to hire them.*
▼

THE NURSE

CHAPTER LXXI

Nursing Recipes for the Sick-Nurse, and Domestic Medicines

Sick Nursing.—All women are likely, at some period of their lives, to be called on to perform the duties of a sick-nurse, and should prepare themselves as much as possible, by observation and reading, for the occasion when they may be required to fulfil the office. The main requirements are good temper, compassion for suffering, sympathy with sufferers (which most women possess), neat-handedness, quiet manners, love of order, and cleanliness. With these qualifications there will be very little to be wished for ; the desire to relieve suffering will inspire a thousand little attentions and surmount the distaste which some of the offices attending the sick-room are apt to create.

Where serious illness visits a household, however, and protracted nursing is likely to become necessary, a professional nurse will probably be engaged who has been trained to her duties. Such nurses may be obtained from the nursing homes in connexion with most of the large hospitals throughout the country. Their usual fee is two to three guineas a week. The advantages of employing such a nurse in cases of serious illness are many. The patient receives every care and attention from one who, by training and experience, has learnt of what attentions such a patient stands most in need. The doctor is helped by having at each visit an accurate report of the patient's condition, the amount of sleep enjoyed, the alterations in the pulse or tempera-ture, etc., since his last visit. He is thus better able to form an opinion

TRAINED NURSES

Until the 1850s most nurses were unskilled and unreliable (Charles Dickens included a nurse of this kind, Sarah Gamp, in his story *Martin Chuzzlewit*). Then Florence Nightingale started her campaign to reform nursing and train women as professional nurses. By the end of the century Frank Mundell was able to write confidently,

> Large numbers of refined and sympathetic women, thoroughly trained in the various duties of their profession, can be summoned almost at a moment's notice to the sick-bed.
> To Florence Nightingale we owe this noble band. She was the first to see the need that existed for trained nurses .... After her return from the Crimea she opened the first training school for nurses with only fifteen probationers [students]. Up to the present time nearly a thousand women have left that institution thoroughly equipped for tending the sick. Now there are also numerous nursing institutions in many of our large towns. (*Heroines of Mercy*, date of publication unknown: about 1900)

Florence Nightingale was the first "heroine of mercy" described in Frank Mundell's book. You probably already know what she had been doing in the Crimea, but if you want to find out more about her life and work you are sure to find books about her in your school and public libraries. Her nursing school was set up at St Thomas's Hospital in London in 1860.

NURSES' PAY, 1876

Nurses might be thought of as a "noble band", but they were not well paid.

> The wages of a probationer at the Birmingham and Midland Counties' Institution . . . are £12 for the first year and £20 for the remaining 2, with board, lodging, and uniform. Probationers must be between 25 and 35. These are the usual terms; but we do not ourselves expect to see nursing widely embraced among women – and especially among gentlewomen – until the terms are improved. A young woman who has to work must begin before 25; a nurse's life is so arduous [hard] that the usual computation allows them twelve years of work, after which time they are incapacitated [unfit]. Is it a career unlikely to tempt a woman of culture, to commence at 25 upon wages which an incompetent servant maid of 18 will not take, and to end her working life – while still in her prime – upon less wages than a head-nurse [i.e. a Nanny] or a "plain cook" can demand and easily obtain? (Article in *Victoria Magazine*, June 1876, quoted in Janet Horowitz Murray, *Strong-Minded Women*, 1982)

Why was a nurse's career likely to be so short? Why, do you think, could nurses not begin training until they were 25? Why would this have discouraged many from taking up the profession?

This statue to a nurse was put up in Walsall in the 1880s. "Sister Dora" was a local heroine: she ran the cottage hospital and nursed the victims of a smallpox epidemic. Her real name was Dorothy Wyndlow Pattison and she was a lady who was inspired by Florence Nightingale's example to take up nursing in spite of family disapproval. She died in 1878.

Good Works

One occupation which was thought suitable for ladies was charitable work. Some rich women thought it a religious duty to visit the poor and help the sick in villages near their country estates. Others became involved in schemes to help those living in the slums of London or other large towns.

EDUCATING THE POOR

Teaching village children, either in Sunday School at the church or by helping in the village school, was a popular activity with conscientious ladies. The school at Little Faringdon was largely financed by the Lady of the Manor, Lady de Mauley. She also took a very active interest in the children and their lessons:

> **1879**
> **May 30. Lady de Mauley visited the school, examined the needlework & gave a fresh supply of material for needlework.**

> **Dec. 19. Lady de Mauley visited the school; gave the children some encouragement about their needlework. She also enquired about their attendance at school.**
> **1880**
> **Jan. Lady de Mauley visited the school on Tuesday & heard the children sing. She commended soft singing & told the children to sing a very little bit softer.**

Lady de Mauley visited regularly throughout the 1880s and 1890s, bringing Lord de Mauley with her most summers to present prizes. Her visits continued until the last mention of her name in the log-book:

> **1897**
> **Sept. 17. No school this afternoon as Lady de Mauley was buried.**
> (*Little Faringdon School Log-Book*, 1879-1900)

You can tell from their elaborate clothes that these are "ladies" and not ordinary elementary schoolteachers, teaching poor children. Can you decide from this picture (1873) how the lesson is going?

HOSPITAL-VISITING

Mrs Gladstone was actively interested in many charities and had bravely visited the London Hospital during an outbreak of cholera in 1866. She encouraged her daughter Mary to visit as well.

1871
London, Mon. Ap. 24
London Hospital with Mama; such interesting cases and marvellous patience with dreadful suffering.
1872
London, Mon. Jan. 22
To the London Hospital by train and cab at 3. Stayed about an hour and a half. Satisfactory on the whole though it is rather shy work somehow going from bed to bed . . . .
London, Mon. Feb. 26
Luncheon at Lucy's [her cousin, Lucy Cavendish; see also p. 9] and with her and Mama at 2 to the London Hospital. We were there 2 hours . . . .(Lucy Masterman, ed., *Mary Gladstone, Diaries and Letters*, 1930)

The London Hospital took poor patients from the East End. Do you think this kind of visiting was valuable? If so, why and to whom? If not, why not?

THE "FASHION FOR YOUNG LADIES . . ."

By the 1860s voluntary work of some kind or another had become a very fashionable activity. In a story in the religious magazine *Sunday at Home* the local vicar criticized girls who dabbled in Sunday school teaching. He explained how it was

> . . . quite the fashion for young ladies, after the excitements of a London season, to take to "schools and poor people", if there be no illness about, and the children are tidy. The pleasure of passing an hour on Sunday in the amiable character of a shepherdess, with a vague idea of doing something a little good . . . does not constitute the material for a good teacher. ("Sunday at Eversfield", *Sunday at Home*, April 1869)

Do you know what the London "season" was? If not, look it up on p. 44.

THE BENEVOLENT FEMALES OF LEEDS

It was not only aristocratic ladies who spent time and effort on working for charity:

> There are in Leeds also two or three clothing societies by which benevolent females of the more opulent and middle classes supply their poor neighbours with garments, which these fair Samaritans make with their own hands. (*Baines' Yorkshire*, 1822)

Why might rich women enjoy this kind of work? Imagine you are living in 1822. Write a letter to persuade a friend to join such a group.

◀ *A popular charitable activity for ladies was organizing holidays and outings for deprived children, like this outing of July 1887.*

New Opportunities

In the second half of the nineteenth century the education of girls improved and there were new jobs available for women.

SECONDARY SCHOOLS FOR GIRLS

Girls from prosperous families began to have the chance of an education rather like the one their brothers received in public or grammar schools. A pupil at Ipswich High School, founded in 1878 as one of a group of schools run by a company that later became the Girls' Public Day Schools' Trust, later remembered how she first went to the school in 1884,

> **... at a time when a High School girl was considered to be the most modern thing alive.... A modern girl, who takes good teaching for granted, can have no idea of the revelation it was to a girl, accustomed to puzzle things out for herself, to be really taught Latin or mathematics, with illustrations and explanations on a blackboard. My home governess had given me an arithmetic book and said: "Read the chapter on decimals and work out the examples as well as you can!" You can imagine the result!** (Memories of Mrs Ethel Palmer, quoted in *G.P.D.S.T. 1872-1972: A Centenary Review*)

This girl was 14 when she first went to school – the extract tells you how she was educated before then.

PARENTS' WORRIES

Subjects like Latin, and Mathematics too, were thought of as "boys subjects". At first girls' schools had to be careful not to alarm parents by including too much academic work like this on the girls'

timetables. At Cheltenham Ladies' College, founded as a boarding and day school for girls in 1854, the headmistress from 1858, Miss Beale, saw that the girls learnt Geometry but never let it be called *Euclid* as it was in boys' schools.

> **The term "Euclid" was never used in College, and long after, in telling of these early struggles, Miss Beale would say ... "Parents thought their daughters would be turned into boys if they learnt Euclid, but they never minded their learning geometry."** (F. Cicely Steadman, *In the Days of Miss Beale*, 1931)

Why do you think parents would worry about their daughters becoming too academic?

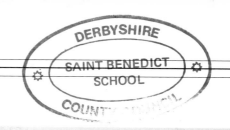

Although women were allowed to study at Oxford and Cambridge from the 1870s, they were not given degrees like men were. (London University, more progressive, was giving women degrees by the 1880s.) This Punch cartoon of 1888 shows how it was feared that the women students would distract the men if more were admitted on equal terms.

How many women can you find running their own ▶ shop or business in Northampton in this group of advertisements of 1888?

BENNETT'S BUSINESS DIRECTORY. ···Advertisements.

W. COOPER,
Wholesale and Retail Fish Merchant,
5, THE GREEN, 16, MARE FAIR, 61, WELLINGBORO ROAD, AND 65, GRAFTON ROAD, NORTHAMPTON. Three Stalls in Markets on Wednesdays and Saturdays.

MISS J. WILLSDON,
Mantle, Costume, and Ladies Outfitting Establishment,
14, THE PARADE, NORTHAMPTON.
Miss J. Willsdon begs to draw the attention of Ladies in the Neighbourhood to the fact that she has always on hand a new and choice assortment of Mantles and Costumes in the latest Paris fashions. Dress and Mantle making on the premises by experienced hands.

THOMAS BECKETT,
LINEN & WOOLLEN DRAPER
43 & 44, Narrow Bridge Street, & 2, Wentworth St,
PETERBOROUGH.

J. E. HALL,
Funeral Director and Coffin Furniture Factor,
30, GROVE ROAD, NORTHAMPTON.

ANN BONHAM & SON,
Cab and Pleasure Brake Proprietors,
NORTHAMPTON.

R. CLEAVER,
WHOLESALE DEALER IN OILS & COLORS
14, WOOD STREET, NORTHAMPTON.

H. BONHAM & SON,
CAB AND CAR PROPRIETORS,
NORTHAMPTON.

A. T. COOPER,
CAB PROPRIETOR, FUNERAL FURNISHER, UNDERTAKER, ETC,
30, WOOD STREET, NORTHAMPTON.

Miss E. BURBIDGE,
CONFECTIONER AND SUGAR BOILER,
Cheltenham House,
7, ST. GILES ST., NORTHAMPTON.

THOS. COSFORD,
BUILDER AND CONTRACTOR,
CONNAUGHT ST., NORTHAMPTON.

BETTER JOBS

In the second half of the nineteenth century clever girls from wealthy families could take examinations at schools like Cheltenham Ladies' College and, by the 1870s, go on to university. You will remember how poorer girls could qualify as elementary schoolteachers (pp. 26-7). There were other opportunities for them, too. In Charlbury, Oxfordshire, C.W. Pumphrey remembered,

> **All through the years of our childhood (1845-1860) the Post Office was managed by two old maids, Miss Walden and her niece . . .**

In the 1890s, Flora Thompson, who wrote *Lark Rise to Candleford*, trained as a Post Office assistant. You can discover another kind of Post Office work open to women in this advertisement:

> **SITUATIONS VACANT: Government Appointments . . . Female Sorters, 30 vacancies, 13 April . . .**
> (*Jackson's Oxford Journal*, 26 March, 1898)

Single women were preferred for jobs like these, and women often had to leave work when they married.

Some local postmistresses combined the work with running a village shop. Other post offices were used for several purposes:

> **Aubrey Miss M., stationer and jet ornament dealer, Prospect St. post office. Servants' registry office.**
> (*Bennett's Business Directory*, Hull, 1888)

Another popular job for women at this time was that of shop assistant (by 1901, 243,000 women worked in shops). Find out what you can about working conditions in shops; books listed on p. 47 will help you.

Women's Rights

Women in nineteenth-century Britain could not be elected to the House of Commons or vote in parliamentary elections. Before 1869, married women could not even own property (anything they had belonged to their husbands). Women could and did campaign for fairer treatment, but it was the men in Parliament who had the power to change things.

By the 1870s women were doing unexpected things – like training to be doctors (Elizabeth Garret Anderson was one of the first to do this; see what you can find out about her from your library).

THE COMING RACE.

Doctor Evangeline. "By the bye, Mr. Sawyer, are you engaged to-morrow afternoon? I have rather a ticklish Operation to perform—an Amputation, you know."
Mr. Sawyer. "I shall be very happy to do it for you."
Dr. Evangeline. "O, no, not THAT! But will you kindly come and administer the Chloroform for me?"

VOTES FOR WOMEN – FOR AND AGAINST

When the 1867 Reform Bill, which gave male householders the vote in the towns, was being discussed in the House of Commons some M.P.s tried to get a vote for women householders too. Though married women would not have been affected by this (who do you think was the "householder" in a married couple's house?), John Stuart Mill argued that all women would benefit if some got the vote:

> ... They [women] would no longer be classed with children, idiots, and lunatics, as incapable of taking care of either themselves or others, and needing that everything should be done for them without asking their consent ...

Mill was one of the 73 M.P.s who supported the giving of the vote to women householders: 196 voted against, agreeing with the following speaker, Mr Laing:

> There were certain things which women could do better than men, and others which they could not do so well. In all that required rough, rude, practical force, stability of character, and intellect, man was superior: whereas in all those relations of life that demanded mildness, softness of character, and amiability [good temper], women far excelled ...
> (*Hansard*, House of Commons Debate, 20 May, 1867)

Do you find Mr Laing's view of women a flattering one or not? See if you can find out when women *did* get the vote in Britain.

PUNCH IMAGINES THE FUTURE

A common way of playing down demands for greater equality between men and women was to make fun of the situations this might lead to.

A WIFE'S RIGHT TO HER PROPERTY

You can see from the following speech in the House of Commons how strong the arguments were for changing the law in order to let married women own property.

> House of Commons, 14 April, 1869
> Mr Russell Gurney
> It is now proposed that for the first time in our history, the property of one-half of the married people of this country should receive the protection of the law .... From the moment of her marriage the wife, in fact, possessed no property; whatever she might up to that time have possessed ... passed from her, and any gift or bequest made to her became at once the property of the husband .... She might be gifted with powers which enabled her to earn an ample fortune, but, the moment it was earned, it was not her's, it was her husband's ... an intelligent police magistrate ... spoke of the numerous cases ... of women, after being left by their husbands, making through their own exertions, their homes comfortable, and finding those homes upset by the return of their husbands, who took possession of the whole of their property ...

Parliament did pass a law to reform this situation – The Married Women's Property Act – in 1869.

Extracts from the Diary of the Coming Woman

Thursday, May 14. Message from Oxford from my youngest sister Bianca to say she had that instant been elected Fellow of Carlyle College. Three hundred and ten competitors .... Bianca's thorough domination of Russian, Japanese, political economy, statistics, aerostatics, electrology, hygiene and thermopeutics, gave her the victory. Hope some day she will stand [as M.P.] for the University ....
Friday, May 15. Busy all the morning preparing my oration on the "Wise Sayings of Wise Women in all Countries and Epochs" for the Congress (interrupted twice by Alfred, who had got the housekeeping accounts ... into a fearful muddle). Great meeting at 3.30 in Emancipation Hall, to welcome Mrs Hale Columbia Spragg, the first female President of the United States ....
Saturday, May 16. Dejeuned [lunched] at the Constellation Hotel ... to meet Mrs President Spragg, Chief Justice Roberta Cokestone ... the Lady Warden of the Cinque Ports, the Lady Mayoress ... and other forward members of the Congress. The President left us at noon. She would balloon over to New York in five hours and a half .... (Punch, 27 January, 1872)

How many things referred to in this imaginary diary would have seemed quite impossible to readers of Punch in 1872? What do you think they would have laughed loudest at? What role is given to the diarist's husband, Alfred? Are there any positions mentioned in the diary as held by women that women have not yet occupied?

Labour-Saving in the Home

By the end of the nineteenth century a few labour-saving devices were available for those families who could afford them.

CLEANING CARPETS

Mrs Beeton's book on household management was first published in 1861. New editions were later published, however, and by the beginning of the next century these were able to take some labour-saving devices almost for granted though, as you can see, the publishers were careful to continue to give advice on the old ways of doing things too.

> **To Sweep a Carpet**
> **The Patent Carpet Sweepers are so effective and cheap that they are now in use everywhere, but where the floor is to be swept with the ordinary broom proceed as follows: before sweeping rooms strew the floor with dried tea-leaves; these will attract the dust.... Light sweeping and soft brooms are desirable ....**

The first really successful carpet-sweepers were American, made from 1876 onwards by the Bissell Carpet Sweeper Company. You can see an example of one of their nineteenth-century sweepers in the Science Museum in London. A similar English model cost 10s. 6d. in 1911.

What machine helps many modern housewives to clean their carpets?

A USEFUL PIECE OF EQUIPMENT

As wives and mothers spent so much time making and altering clothes for the family, a machine first invented by the American Isaac Singer in 1851 was very welcome (has the name of the inventor already told you what this was?) The writer Kathleen Ashby remembered how her mother, a domestic servant, had saved up for a similar machine when she was engaged to be married in the 1880s:

> **Hannah ... had also to save money for a sewing-machine – a Jones, made of iron and steel, which fifty years later was still capable of use.** (M.K. Ashby, *Joseph Ashby of Tysoe*, 1961)

Hannah would have had to save up about £4 or £5, about half one year's salary.

By the later nineteenth century, prosperous families had gas piped into their homes. Some gas fires, and cooking stoves like this one, were on the market. The labour of heaving coal around and of carefully watching a coal fire used to heat an oven was reduced in households with a gas cooker. (You can see this 1864 cooker in the Castle Museum, York.)

Which useful, labour-saving device is shown in this picture of 1900? Can you work out how the power is being provided for it? You can see a machine like this in the Science Museum in London.

▼

THE VALUE OF THE FAMILY SEWING MACHINE

A miner born in 1892 at Birtley in Durham later remembered how useful his mother had found her sewing machine:

> **Mother was a gentle little woman . . . . She was thrifty [careful with money] and knew how to sew, knit, and could easily operate a Singer sewing machine. Although there was no gas or electric light in our home she would pedal that machine under the light of an oil lamp. We, therefore, were assured of warm underclothing in the winter, made up from material bought . . . from shop sales.** (Thomas Jordan, unpublished autobiography, quoted in John Burnett, ed., *Useful Toil*, 1974)

Can you work out what type of sewing machine this was? Notice an improvement that has taken place in lighting, even in ordinary working people's homes, by the 1890s: what is Mrs Jordan using to light her work instead of a candle?

Fashion

Women's fashions changed a good deal during the nineteenth century, as you can see from the illustrations in this book. Rich women could afford the very latest styles in expensive materials. However, poorer women were also interested in clothes and tried to make their "Sunday best" as fashionable as they could.

BUYING BONNETS

Elizabeth Wordsworth, a clergyman's daughter, wrote a letter from London to her sister in the country in 1866 full of fashion news.

> ... Pris and I got some bonnets at Gomm & Harts, in a style of great simplicity, for fear of corrupting the minds of our Sunday Scholars at Stanford – hers to be white straw and mine white aerophane, both trimmed with pink crape .... Priscilla got herself a new hat and white feather .... (Letter 3 May, 1866, quoted in Georgina Battiscombe, *Reluctant Pioneer*, 1978)

Can you work out where these bonnets were going to be worn?

You could buy a false fringe like this one for 10s. 6d. in 1895.

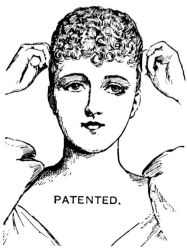

PATENTED.

A SCOTTISH WOMAN KEEPS UP WITH THE FASHIONS

James Barrie admired the way that his mother managed to make fashionable clothes for her daughters despite the family's poverty.

> Never was a woman with such an eye for [fashion]. She had no fashion plates [coloured pictures]; she did not need them. The minister's wife (a cloak), the banker's daughters (the new sleeve) – they had but to pass our window once, and the scalp, so to speak, was in my mother's hands. Observe her rushing, scissors in hand, thread in mouth, to the drawers where her daughters' Sabbath [Sunday] clothes were kept .... (J.M. Barrie, *Margaret Ogilvy*, 1896)

SUITABLE DRESS FOR SERVANTS

Maids generally wore uniform while at work, but their leisure outfits were often restricted too. Flora Thompson remembered how when servants went to church they

> ... had to leave their best hats with the red roses and ostrich tips in the boxes under their beds and "make frights of themselves" in funny little flat bonnets. When the Princess of Wales, afterwards Queen Alexandra, set the fashion of wearing the hair in a curled fringe over the forehead, and the fashion spread until it became universal, a fringe was forbidden to maids. They must wear their hair brushed straight back from their brows. A great hardship. (Flora Thompson, *Lark Rise to Candleford*, 1939)

You can find an example of an employer who objected to fringes on p. 19.

Fashionable ladies dressed like this at the beginning of the nineteenth century.

A lady's day-dress of 1835. Find out how a lady made her waist so small. How have fashions changed since the early years of the century? Look for examples of late Victorian fashions and make some sketches of changing skirt shapes (see p. 31 and p. 43).

▼

PRAISING THE NATURAL LOOK

Respectable girls did not wear make-up. However, there were various ways in which they made themselves look more attractive and some even dared to redden their cheeks with rouge. *Punch* printed some verses on this subject in 1869:

> ### A Sensible Young Person
> 'Tis not because she dresses well
>   That I admire Miss BROWN:
> Let other tongues her toilettes tell,
>   I cannot note them down.
>
> Nor is it from her talents that
>   My admiration springs;
> Although I hear that she can "tat"
>   As sweetly as she sings.
>
> 'Tis that no other charms she'll wear
>   Than those by nature grown:
> Her cheeks are paintless, and her hair
>   I'm told, is all her own.

Pretend you are a country girl in nineteenth-century Britain. How would you get information about changes in fashion? Think of as many different ways as you can.

Amusements

Ladies were expected to have "accomplishments", and these included being able to sing and play the piano. Such skills helped to provide amusement in the home. Working people also enjoyed singing. For people living in towns, there were theatres and music-halls to visit; country people depended on making their own entertainment.

VALUABLE ACCOMPLISHMENTS

Cicely Steadman explained how a wealthy Victorian girl was trained to "decorate her home and entertain her guests". This meant that

. . . girls gave much time to the piano,

harp, violin and singing, to drawing, sketching, painting on various materials such as china, satin and American cloth, to plain sewing, different kinds of embroidery, and to such forms of lace-making as crochet, tatting, and netting. (F. Cicely Steadman, *In the Days of Miss Beale*, 1931)

Have you got any of these skills? Would you have been able to occupy yourself happily as a young Victorian lady? You may have seen examples of Victorian lace or fancy-work — perhaps there are some pieces at home, or in your grandparents' house. If not, your local museum may have some.

This young lady of the 1880s is riding, like Mary Gladstone, in Hyde Park, London. She is riding side-saddle: it was not thought proper for women to ride astride. Who, until 1987, rode side-saddle once a year in London?
▼

SONGS AND SINGERS

Girls sang at parties, or to entertain their families in the evenings. Some women became professional singers and composers: the very popular song "In the Gloaming" was written by Annie Fortescue Harrison, and sold over 140,000 copies in 10 years.

Look out for old copies of Victorian songs – if you are lucky you can sometimes find these at jumble sales. If you enjoy singing make up a programme for a Victorian musical evening. Study the words of the songs: what are the favourite subjects?

MUSIC HALLS

In the second half of the nineteenth century music halls became popular, and places where women as well as men could go for an evening's entertainment. Sentimental and funny songs were both enjoyed. Sometimes the humour was rather black, as in the following song (what is the really sad story that it is telling?).

> There was I, waiting at the church,
> Waiting at the church, waiting at the
> church,
> When I found he'd left me in the lurch,
> Lor! How it did upset me!
> All at once he sent a little note,
> Here's the very note, and this is what he
> wrote:
> Can't get away to marry you today,
> My wife won't let me!

◀ Lady cyclists in Battersea Park, 1895. Cycling was a popular pastime for women by the late nineteenth century: some girls wore short skirts or even trousers called "bloomers", or "rationals", when they cycled.

LONDON AMUSEMENTS FOR RICH AND POOR

As the daughter of a famous politician, Mary Gladstone was often asked to parties and had many outings. She preferred concerts and theatre visits to balls, however.

> **1872**
> **London, Mon. June 24. A rush all day.**
> **Ride at 12 . . . . To Lambeth afternoon,**
> **tea with Stephy and hurry home, snack**
> **of food and off to . . . Concert . . . . Superb**
> **programme . . . . Rushed home and**
> **dressed for the ball – a trial, only a short**
> **time there . . . .** (Lucy Masterman, ed.,
> *Mary Gladstone, Diary and Letters*, 1930)

Walter Besant, writing an article on "The Amusements of the People" in 1884, felt that ordinary women had very few amusements outside the home:

> **Certainly one can see a few of them any**
> **Sunday walking about in the lanes and**
> **fields of northern London, with their**
> **lovers; in the evening they may also be**
> **observed having tea in the tea-gardens.**
> **These, however, are the better sort of**
> **girls; they are well-dressed, and**
> **generally quiet in their behaviour. The**
> **domestic servants, for the most part,**
> **spend their "evening out" in taking tea**
> **with other servants, whose evening is**
> **in . . . . When women are married and**
> **the cares of maternity set in, one does**
> **not see how they can get any holiday or**
> **recreation at all . . . .** (*Contemporary*
> *Review*, 1884)

Why does Walter Besant only talk about amusements on Sunday? Here, of course, he is studying the steady, "respectable" women: in very poor areas women as well as men went to public houses.

Women's Reading

Though some women loved to read serious books, light reading was considered "suitable" for them. Many magazines were produced for women readers in the nineteenth century. At first, these were chiefly for leisured ladies, but as education improved and more working women learnt to read, magazines started to cater for them, too. A large number of "family magazines" were also published, some especially for Sunday reading. Novels were popular with women of all ranks, though certain topics were thought "unsuitable". When Mrs Gaskell wrote a book in 1853 about an unmarried mother she was horrified to hear that two local fathers of families had actually burnt their copies "and a third has forbidden his wife to read it".

NOVELETTES

Cheap paper-covered books were available by the 1880s even for village women.

> Several of the hamlet women took in one of these weekly, as published, for the price was but one penny, and these were handed round until the pages were thin and frayed with use. Copies of others found their way there from neighbouring villages, or from daughters in service, and there was always quite a library of them in circulation.
> The novelette of the 'eighties was a romantic love story, in which the poor governess always married the duke....
> (Flora Thompson, *Lark Rise to Candleford*, 1939)

Can you suggest examples of modern "stories for women" like these novelettes?

TOO MANY ROMANTIC NOVELS

At the beginning of the century Jane Austen wrote a very funny book about a young heroine who had read so many novels that she expected life to be like them – men to be heroes of romance, old houses to be full of mysteries and ghosts, etc. (you can find *Northanger Abbey* in your public library). In the 1890s a writer of improving books for young people complained:

> Now-a-days, I am afraid, ideas of life, and all that life brings of joy and sorrow, are too often taken by girls from books. And as so many of these books are not drawn from the life, the actual experience of maidens from eighteen to five and twenty is apt to fall flat by comparison.
> There are many exceptions to this rule, and we cannot be too grateful to those authors who first provided wholesome romances for the young .... But we cannot be blind to the danger that exists in these days, when a perfect torrent of stories passes from the press, encouraging by florid descriptions of dress and surroundings, and sensational situations ... a false view of life, so that the girls who are allowed to read any book that comes in their way, are unfitted for everyday duties, instead of being braced for them ....
> (Emma Marshall, *Fine Gold or Ravenswood Courtenay*, undated, but probably published in the 1890s)

What are the dangers according to Emma Marshall of reading too much romantic fiction?

Women's magazines showed the latest styles. These ball-dresses (with crinolines – skirts spread out over hoops) appeared in 1862. Can you find the name of the magazine? ▶

MAGAZINES

Typical of the magazines published for poorer women was one started in 1848 – *The Family Economist; A Penny Monthly Magazine For The Industrious Classes*. It declared itself to be

> ... devoted to the Moral, Physical and Domestic Improvement of the Industrious Classes ... containing original articles by the Best Writers on Domestic Economy, Education, Sanitary Reform, Cottage Gardening, Farming, Social Sketches, Moral Tales, Family Secrets and Valuable Household recipes. (Quoted in Irene Dancyger, *A World of Women*, 1978)

In 1852, Mr S.O. Beeton (whose wife wrote the famous cookery book) published *The Englishwoman's Domestic Journal*, price 2d. a month, which had a circulation of 50,000 a month by 1856. This, too, had recipes, household hints, articles on serious subjects, serial stories and also included fashion news.

Use the material in this book to make up some pages of a magazine for women of, say, the 1880s. Remember to check styles of dress carefully for any illustrations – and dates of anything you advertise for sale.

Not all women just read novelettes. This photograph of about 1875 shows a Welsh grandmother with her Bible beside her.
▼

THE FASHIONS
Expressly designed and prepared for the
Englishwoman's Domestic Magazine.
FEBRUARY 186

Difficult Words

aerostatics	the science of air-pressure and gases.
amiable	pleasant.
black lead	a polish used on iron grates to give them a smooth, black finish.
brake	a horse-drawn wagon where passengers sat facing each other.
bustle	a pad or framework under a skirt to push it out at the back.
buttermilk	the liquid left behind after milk has been churned into butter.
certificated teacher, second class	a teacher who had passed the examinations for pupil-teachers, but who had not trained at a college.
conservatory	a glasshouse for plants built on to a house.
Crimea, the	a Russian peninsula, on the Black Sea, where England and France fought a war against Russia in the 1850s.
draper's	a shop selling cloth, sewing materials, etc.
ganger	the foreman of a gang of labourers.
infirmary	hospital.
junket	a milk pudding.
mantle	a loose, sleeveless coat.
middlemen	dealers who gave out material to home workers and sold the finished work.
progeny	children.
Quaker	the name given to members of the Religious Society of Friends founded in the seventeenth century by George Fox. Quakers dressed very simply and broke with many of the conventions of the Christian Church.
Season, the London	period between May and July when fashionable families moved up to their London homes and entertained each other in a constant round of parties and balls.
situation	a job.
strew, to	throw down, scatter.
tat, to tat	knot thread into a kind of lace.
trousseau	a collection of clothes ready for a girl's marriage.
wedding portion	money or property taken by a girl to her husband when they married.

Money

Money

There were 12 old pence (d.) in a shilling (s.) and 20 shillings in a pound (£). A shilling is equal to 5p.

Prices seem very low, but remember that wages were too. Don't compare prices with those of today, without looking at earnings then and now.

44

Date List

1815 Battle of Waterloo: end of the Napoleonic wars with France.

1834 Poor Law Amendment Act: women as well as men were affected by this. Able-bodied people who could not support themselves had to go into workhouses.

A sad story goes with this family photograph of the 1870s. The young husband and wife emigrated from South Wales to the U.S.A., where better jobs could be had. Jane, the wife, fell ill with tuberculosis and was homesick for her mother and sisters. Her husband sent for them, but when they arrived after a long sea voyage, Jane was dead.

Has your family any nineteenth-century photographs? If not, your local library many have some.

1837 Queen Victoria came to the throne.

1842 Mines Act: women (and young children) were no longer allowed to work underground.

1847 Ten Hour Act: women and all under 18 were not to work more than ten hours a day in textile factories.

1854 Cheltenham Ladies College founded: a public (boarding) school for girls.

1854-6 War with Russia in the Crimea. Florence Nightingale went out to nurse the wounded.

1867 Manchester Women's Suffrage Committee founded to campaign for votes for women.

1869 Girton College founded to give girls higher education. It moved to Cambridge in 1873.
Married Women's Property Act passed by Parliament.

1870 Education Act set up Board schools, which meant more girls as well as more boys received elementary education.
Women with property could vote for members of school boards, and even be elected themselves.

1872 Girls' Public Day School Company (now Girls' Public Day School Trust) founded to set up secondary schools for girls.

1875 Women could be elected as Poor Law Guardians.
The first women attended the Trades Union Congress.

1879 Lady Margaret Hall, first woman's college at Oxford, founded.

1897 Various suffrage groups, pressing for votes for women, amalgamated to become the National Union of Women's Suffrage Societies.

1901 Death of Queen Victoria.

45

Places to Visit

There are many museums which have displays of nineteenth-century costume and domestic articles. Country houses, too provide interesting information on the life of the rich – and of their servants. The following lists give a selection of such places.

Museums

Bath The Museum of Costume.

Cardiff (near) The Welsh Folk Museum, St Fagan's (a costume collection, and a number of cottages and farmhouses, several with nineteenth-century furniture and cooking equipment).

London Geffrye Museum, Shoreditch (period rooms including nineteenth century).
National Museum of Labour History, Limehouse Town Hall, Commercial Road, London E1 (pictures and information about the lives and work of poor women).
The Museum of London, London Wall (life in nineteenth-century London).
Victoria and Albert Museum, South Kensington (costume and furniture).

Manchester Gallery of English Costume.

Norwich Strangers' Hall (Victorian rooms and cooking equipment).

Nottingham Brewhouse Yard Museum (furnished rooms).
Museum of Costume and Textiles.

Oxford Museum of Oxford (Victorian cottage-kitchen).

York The Castle Museum (Victorian rooms).

Houses

Claydon House, Buckinghamshire (relics of Florence Nightingale and the bedroom she used when she visited her sister).

Erddig, near Wrexham, Wales (Victorian laundries, kitchen equipment, pictures of servants).

Hughenden Manor, High Wycombe, Buckinghamshire (home of Disraeli, a Victorian Prime Minister, and his wife; much Victorian furniture).

Osborne House, Isle of Wight (a favourite home of Queen Victoria).

BOOKS FOR YOUNGER READERS

Sheila Ferguson, *Growing Up in Victorian Britain*, B.T. Batsford, 1977, reprinted 1984, and other titles in the *Growing Up* series

Gladys Cuddeford, *Women and Society*, Hamish Hamilton, 1967

Sarah Harris, *History in Focus: Women At Work*, B.T. Batsford, 1981

J. Hughes, *Victorian Sunday*, Wayland, 1972

Crispin Paine and John Rhodes, *The Worker's Home*, Oxfordshire Museums Service, 1979

Michael Rawcliffe, *Finding Out About Victorian Country Life*, B.T. Batsford, 1984, *Finding Out About Victorian Social Reformers*, B.T. Batsford, 1987, and other titles in the *Finding Out About* series.

Jennifer Ruby, *Costume in Context: The Victorians*, B.T. Batsford, 1987

Marion Sichel, *Costume Reference: The Regency* and *The Victorians*, B.T. Batsford, 1978, and other titles in the *Costume Reference* series

P.P. Speed, *Learning and Teaching in Victorian Times*, Longman, and other titles in the *Then and There* series.

N.B. Some museums produce very good information sheets, such as Oxfordshire Museums' Information sheets 14 (Kitchen Utensils) and 15 (Cleaning and Laundry Work). These are quite cheap and can be bought in museums in Oxfordshire and in the Museum of Oxford, St Aldate's, Oxford.

BOOKS FOR OLDER READERS

John Burnett, *Useful Toil*, Penguin, 1982

C. Cunnington and Phyllis Willett, *Handbook of English Costume in the Nineteenth Century*, Faber, 1959

Irene Dancyger, *A World of Women*, Gill & Macmillan, 1978

Margaret Llewelyn Davies, ed., *Life as We Have Known It*, Hogarth Press 1931, republished Virago, 1977.

Vanda Foster, *A Visual History of Costume: The Nineteenth Century*, B.T. Batsford, 1984

Henry Mayhew, *London Labour and the London Poor*, 1861

Janet Horowitz Murray, *Strong-minded Women*, Penguin, 1984

F.K. Prochaska, *Women and Philanthropy in Nineteenth-century England*, O.U.P., 1980

Flora Thompson, *Lark Rise to Candleford*, O.U.P., 1939

Doreen Yarwood, *Five Hundred Years of Technology in the Home*, B.T. Batsford, 1983

Doreen Yarwood, *The British Kitchen*, B.T. Batsford, 1981

N.B. Useful extracts from documents of the period can be found in the *Human Documents* series, ed. E. Royston Pike, Allen & Unwin – e.g. "Human Documents of the Industrial Revolution", 1966.

A middle-class family at home, 1900. Piano-playing and singing were considered desirable accomplishments for young ladies in the nineteenth century.

Index

(*Numbers in italic indicate pages on which illustrations occur.*)